CHOICEABLES®

CHOICEABLES®

A simple and profound new model to
help make the best choices in life and business

ANDREA DEFRIES

For everyone making choices

Wherever the mind wanders, restless in its search for satisfaction without, go within. Train it to rest in the Self.

Bhagavad-Gita

"The Choiceables Model helped me reflect on my thoughts and processes. It guided me to access my creative energy and separate myself from the business. I now have a refined business plan that links my vision and values with my objectives that is exciting and practical. I loved the model – it really works."

Dr Elizabeth Jordan, Systemic and Organisational Consultant

"Wisdom, charm and strategy."

Reina James-Reinstein, Author

"The Choiceables Model is a great toolkit for discussion. It enabled me to consider what choices are important to me now, why, and what I am going to do next."

Helen Morgan, Business Coach

"In Choiceables, Andrea offers an elegant, encouraging, and practical model for exploring how we make choices. Within a few days of reading this beautiful book, I have already noticed a subtle, gentle shift in my choice-making processes."
Natalie Jameson, Consultant

"Thought provoking and lovingly arranged, with powerful techniques to help make choices."
Colin Brown, former British Film Commissioner

"I often think I am in the process of, and not in the completing. The structure of the Choiceables Model helped me to consider the most important choices and make them. I feel much better now I have a clear strategy and action plan."
Zena Rogers, Health and Wellbeing Consultant

contents

Introduction
An overview of the three steps in the Choiceables Model
A visual of the Choiceables Model

Practical exercises to help you make choices
Gratitude
A final word about the Choiceables Model
About Andrea Defries

Introduction

Our choices drive our lives. Yet, do we ever consider the best way to make choices?

For more than twenty years, as a business consultant and coach, I have helped leaders to make choices.

I have also spent many years learning from spiritual teachers and have seen how they are able to be within and receive direction.

I have written this book from this fusion of spiritual learning and business experience, helping to shine a light on how to make choices.

It is a step-by-step guide that shares with you a simple, but also profound way to make the best choices for your business and your life.

Until now, there has been no word for making the many choices we make daily; some trivial, some life-changing.

I call it Choiceables.

Welcome to the Choiceables® Model.

Best choices = best life and business

Enjoy!

Choices shape our lives and businesses

When we have to make an important choice, it can be stressful. Sometimes it can be a simple yes or no; sometimes there are so many choices that we become confused. Sometimes the choices appear to be made for us.

Often the more we think about our choices, the more frightening it becomes. What if it goes wrong, what if I lose money, what if the job does not work out, what if I do not like it?

We can make a choice and get the outcome we wanted.

We can make a choice and then think we should have made a different choice.

We can make a choice and it opens up opportunities we never dreamed of.

Whatever choice we make, we can choose how to manage it, and we can always make another choice.

Each choice leads us into another life or business situation.

Sometimes it is better to wait and not make a choice.

However, that is a choice.

When we make an important choice, we should not leave any stone unturned.

This model is a simple and profound way to help you make any choice.

A question

There are more than seven billion people on the planet. Research has demonstrated that every day, each of us has thousands of thoughts. Many of these thoughts are about making choices. This is a staggering amount of choices.

Can you remember what you thought about 15 minutes ago, 10 minutes ago, 5 minutes ago, 1 minute ago?

We cannot remember many of our thoughts and yet they drive our choices and our choices shape our lives.

It is our thoughts that drive our choices, and our choices define our lives and businesses.

Watch your thoughts,

they become words.

Watch your words,

they become actions.

Watch your actions,

they become habits.

Watch your habits,

they become character.

Watch your character,

it becomes your destiny.

Lao Tzu

An overview of the three steps in the Choiceables Model

The model is designed in three steps. You can use each step separately, blend different aspects of the steps, or use all three steps together as one choice-making process. It is not fixed. It depends on your specific need.

The steps will be explained in detail in the book.

I AM THE BEST
AT THIS

I NEED A
BETTER JOB

THERE IS NEVER
ENOUGH TIME

THE MANAGERS
ARE BRILLIANT

I AM NOT
GOOD ENOUGH

Looking inside and reflecting

Looking inside, we use what I call mind-bricks.
These are the thoughts and feelings that influence
our choices.

Looking outside and questioning

Questioning around the SPECS Framework

The SPECS Framework is made up of the only five considerations you need when you want to make a choice. The framework is a key element of the Choiceables Model. It enables a shortcut to ensure you have thought of what is the most important before you make your choice.

The first letter of the only five considerations creates the mnemonic **SPECS**

Self-confidence

Processing

Expression

Connectivity

Security

Each of these concepts are explained thoroughly later in the book. You can consider all the words in the SPECS Framework or select those that are most relevant and/or important to you.

Being within

This step is less about external action and more about the inner world of being within. When we are being within, we are not constantly thinking and doing.

Guiding principles to consider when making your choices

Be open

Be positive

Be kind to yourself and others

Be patient

Listen

THE CHOICEABLES MODEL

looking inside	looking outside	being within
reflect	question	be
thinking		beyond thinking

MIND-BRICKS

The bricks that make up your life now. Your thoughts, feelings, memories, conditioning. Your personality.

Choices are made according to your mind-bricks.

SPECS FRAMEWORK

Self-confidence
Processing
Expression
Connectivity
Security

The only five considerations for making any choice.

BEING WITHIN

Focusing on being within, beyond thought, where there is an inner stillness and knowing.

Being within, choices are clear.

STEP ONE

MIND-BRICKS

The bricks that make
up your life now.
Your thoughts,
feelings, memories,
conditioning.
Your personality.

Choices are made
according to your
mind-bricks.

Why we build mind-bricks

There we are, cosy and secure within our mother's womb, and suddenly we are separated—we are alone—we are confused, we are probably in shock. We are born.

However, humans are naturally disposed to adapt and protect themselves. To be safe, we build a wall of mind-bricks around ourselves driven by fear, safety and the desire to be happy.

What are mind-bricks?

Each mind-brick is a thought, feeling, desire, fear, habit, like, or dislike. We also have access to the bricks of imagination, conditioning, memory, image, and events in our life and our reactions to them.

When we are told we are talented, excellent, helpful, kind, or beautiful, the positive-thinking bricks are built.

When we are ignored, do not get what we want, or are told we are bad, then the anger, rejection, shame, or guilt bricks are built.

The more we build positive mind-bricks, the more we are likely to make positive choices.

Think good and good will happen.

Spiritual Teacher

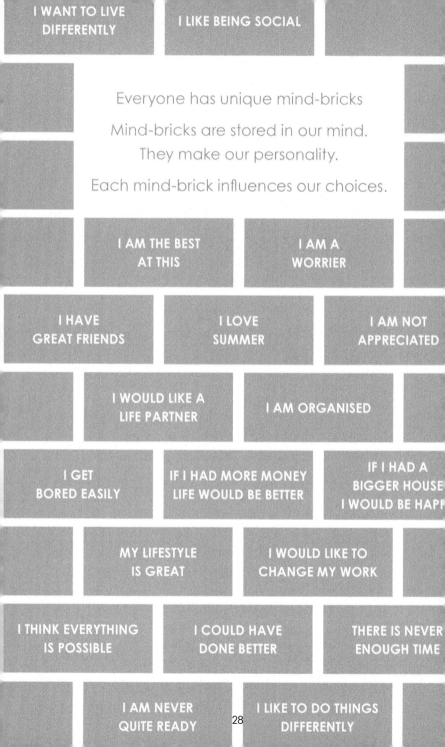

I WANT TO LIVE DIFFERENTLY

I LIKE BEING SOCIAL

Everyone has unique mind-bricks

Mind-bricks are stored in our mind.
They make our personality.

Each mind-brick influences our choices.

I AM THE BEST AT THIS

I AM A WORRIER

I HAVE GREAT FRIENDS

I LOVE SUMMER

I AM NOT APPRECIATED

I WOULD LIKE A LIFE PARTNER

I AM ORGANISED

I GET BORED EASILY

IF I HAD MORE MONEY LIFE WOULD BE BETTER

IF I HAD A BIGGER HOUSE I WOULD BE HAPP

MY LIFESTYLE IS GREAT

I WOULD LIKE TO CHANGE MY WORK

I THINK EVERYTHING IS POSSIBLE

I COULD HAVE DONE BETTER

THERE IS NEVER ENOUGH TIME

I AM NEVER QUITE READY

I LIKE TO DO THINGS DIFFERENTLY

28

Conditioning appears to be true

A 90-year-old lady told me that when she was nine, her teacher said she would not come to anything. That one sentence, from the millions of sentences she heard in her life, was continually remembered. It made her feel 'not good enough' a feeling many of us share.

This feeling drove her to want to be the best she could be, but it also made her anxious. When you think you are not good enough, it is because you tend to think there is someone better than you. The teacher did not realise the impact of her words, but she sat on the lady's shoulder for many years until that lady learned to let go of the 'not good enough' mind-brick.

Throughout our lives, we all experience similar conditioning. Positive and negative comments, which often say more about the person giving them than about the person receiving them. Yet we can retain these experiences in our mind as though they are true and allow them to influence us for a whole lifetime.

Conditioning is a major influence on our choices.

The desire wheel

Most desires come from our mind bricks and these influence our choices. We desire something because we think something is missing. If we had more money and a bigger house, or a new client, or a different country, we would be happy. Some desires need to be fulfilled and others may not.

We can reflect on why we have these desires. Sometimes we have desire to compensate for a deeper need that seems unfulfilled. This could be a need to be heard, recognised, loved. Some desires are a habit.

When we think the desire is fulfilled, we have a short period of time when we believe ourselves to be happy. Soon the mind gets hooked on wanting again because it is rarely satisfied and wants to repeat the feeling of a desire fulfilled.

We are running on a desire wheel, which we may not be able to stop.

Many of our choices are made because of our desires.

Notice how desire influences your choices.

Man's many desires are like the small metal coins he carries around in his pocket. The more he has, the more they weigh him down.

Sathya Sai Baba

The pattern of future and past thinking

Many of our mind-bricks are in a pattern that makes us:

feel anxious about the future; and

worry about the past.

Thinking about the past and future does not allow a clear mind to consider the choice as it is now in the present.

Although we can learn from past experiences, circumstances were different in the past, and we do not know what will happen in the future.

Notice whether your choices are influenced by past and future thinking and take this into consideration when making your choices.

Notice how thinking about the past and future influences your choices.

What is the impact of mind-bricks?

Our mind-bricks are constantly changing and it seems we have no lasting happiness or inner peace.

Yet much of our thinking has developed into a changing and repetitive pattern that we recognise, like the image of a record going around and around that we cannot stop.

Life seems like a constant play of happy—unhappy—happy, and on it goes for a lifetime. Usually we try to make choices to make us feel happier, more successful, and protected.

As we mature, we realise some of these mind-bricks we have carefully nurtured are not really protecting us, but are actually blocking us. These types of mind-bricks can influence our choices and sometimes it means we do not make the best choices.

Mind-bricks can allow the light to come in and the light to go out.

Mind-bricks can also block the light coming in and the light going out.

Business mind-bricks

Every business has its unique mind-bricks. These can come from many places including the following.

- Vision and purpose
- Perception of the brand
- Processes and systems
- What is working well and what is not
- The owner's background and desires
- Leadership and management styles
- The skills of the employees
- The types of clients and relationships
- The added value the company offers
- Stakeholder influence
- The level of trust people have in the company
- The financial situation
- What the key decision makers want to do and how
- Governance
- Products and services

Each mind-brick influences business choices.

Notice which bricks are helpful for your choices and notice which bricks are not.

Prioritising is a choice

We prioritise to order our tasks. When we do not act on the priority, it is usually because it is the most difficult or least enjoyable task. This resistance is because of our mind-bricks. Successful leaders are clear about their choice of priorities and follow through. When making a choice, ask yourself, what are your priorities?

Attachment mind-bricks

We all have attachments; some we recognise and some we do not. These attachments affect our choices because we do not want them to change. For example, when a leader is attached to a product even though it is not profitable, it will be difficult to remove that product.

When partners start a business and are attached to each other, but find over time they have different ideas and do not work well together, it is difficult to choose to separate. When people are attached to working in a certain way and have particular behaviours, it is difficult to change.

When you are making your choices, make sure you consider your attachments. You may need to let go of some attachments to make better choices.

Notice your attachments because they affect your choices.

Values bricks

In my experience, clients with clear values, that are truly lived, tend to make better choices and be more susccessful.

This is because there is clarity around what is important and that does not change, whatever the choices.

For instance, if a client has the value of integrity, everything in the business needs to have integrity.

It is not easy to embed values into a business because everyone in the business has to understand them and make choices aligned with them.

Whether it is around recruiting people, designing service delivery, creating a board or senior management team, or developing a new business plan, it has to align with the company's values.

These values underpin the culture of the business.

The best choices need to be aligned with values.

Examples of values for individuals

- Trust
- Integrity
- Curiosity
- Fun
- Honesty
- Recognition
- Freedom
- Kindness
- Health
- Abundance
- Courage
- Happiness
- Truth
- Wisdom
- Balance
- Drive
- Achievement
- Empathy

Examples of values for business

- Innovation and creativity
- Integrity
- A sense of fun
- Being yourself
- Nurture and support
- Adding value
- Motivating others
- Delivering excellence
- Continual learning
- Respecting each other
- Listening to others
- High performing
- Team work
- Taking responsibility
- Dedication
- Value for money
- Delivering on time and in budget
- Efficiency
- Honesty and fairness
- Openness and transparency

How to identify your company's core values

- ○ Discuss with your staff and major stakeholders what they think the company's core values are. This can be done at meetings, in focus groups or online. Decide on a small team and agree the company's three to six core values. Ensure they can be understood and remembered.
- ○ Provide clear sentences to explain what the values actually mean in practice.
- ○ When making important business choices, ensure the choices are aligned with the company's core values.

This process will check the choice 'fits' with the company's specific culture.

Regularly review your values to ensure they remain relevant.

Who and what knocks your mind-bricks?

Frequently, we find ourselves in a situation where we want to keep some of our bricks and get rid of others.

If we become angry, it is because we have an anger brick inside our mind. When we have anxiety, jealousy, or anger bricks, we often want to remove them because they make us and others feel upset.

But we worry that if we take down a lot of bricks, our wall might collapse and there will be no protection.

If we notice when our bricks are knocked and we are upset or we upset others, then we can change them. Even a small change will make a difference.

Life knocks our mind-bricks again and again. Sometimes even when we think we have removed the mind-brick, we find the brick still exists because it is still there to be knocked. This can happen when we think we are no longer angry and yet an event occurs and we find our anger returns.

The mind-bricks that are knocked can influence our choices.

To make the best choices, notice which bricks are knocked and why.

The mind is everything. What you think you become.

Buddha

How to do step one

Looking inside and reflecting

Your mind-brick wall

To begin, write down what choice you want to make and why. Then write down the mind-bricks of thoughts and feelings you have about that choice.

If there are patterns, notice them. Similar bricks can be grouped together for simplicity and focus. Sticky notes are useful for this purpose. Keep to the main mind-bricks, so you can manage the information easily. This will help you reflect and receive insight on what is influencing your choices.

Values

Your values are key to making choices. They do not change whatever choices are made. The best choices are aligned with values. You can have individual and business values as described previously. Identify and write down your three to six key values.

The Choiceables activity checklist

Why	Why are you making this choice?	Before making a choice
Outcome	What outcome do you want from this choice?	
Critical success factors (CSF)	What are the critical factors that would make this choice successful?	During the process of making a choice
Activities	What activities will be required if you make this choice?	
Impact	What impact will this choice have on other aspects of the business or your life?	
Resources	What resources do you need if you make this choice? Is it feasible?	
Measures of success	What are your measures of a successful choice?	
Review and improve	Review the choice to see whether it is working or not	After the choice has been made

The list of Choiceables

Listing your choices will help make sure you make the choices you need to make. It will also help you to consider the choices you do **not** need to make. You may choose to do this with your team, friends or family. Here is an example of how you can list the choices in a table.

Date	Choiceables to be made now	Choiceables to be made today	Choiceables to be made this week	Choiceables to be made this month	Choiceables to be made this quarter

STEP TWO

SPECS FRAMEWORK

Self-confidence
Processing
Expression
Connectivity
Security

The only five
considerations for
making any choice.

What is the SPECS Framework?

The SPECS Framework contains the only five considerations you need to make a choice. It can be used in many ways, specifically to reflect on you about you, about you in relationships, and as a business tool.

- To use for yourself to make choices
- For you to coach other people to make choices
- For someone to coach you to make choices
- As a framework for individuals and teams to use consistently across the business

Types of questions

- Closed questions – require yes or no answers
- Open questions – allow the responder to explore
- Loaded questions – expect a particular answer
- Memory questions – go back to the past
- Analytical questions – enable thought and analysis
- Rhetorical questions – do not require an answer

Questions help to identify and explore

- Opportunities
- Needs
- Outcomes
- Anxieties
- Perspectives
- Anticipation/fears
- Planning
- Wants
- What is working well
- Likes
- What is not working well
- Clarification
- Predictions
- Evaluation
- Resources
- Past experiences
- Actions to take
- Building on ideas
- Completing
- History
- Motivation
- Implementation
- What is stopping or blocking
- Integration
- Ideas
- Conflict
- New approaches
- Risks

Examples of open questions

- What is stopping you from making the choice?
- What is confusing you?
- What else do you need to know?
- Who else can help you?
- If you could have all the resources you want, what would you do now?
- If you could start again, what would you do differently?
- What is worrying you?
- What is motivating you?
- What will help you make this choice?
- In what ways could your plan go wrong?
- What if it does not work out?
- What is your plan A, B, C?
- What do you need to stop doing so you can make this choice?

You can ask questions around the SPECS Framework to reflect on the outcome of past choices, to consider the choices you need to make now, and to investigate the choices you might make in the future.

Learn from the past

- Consider aspects of the SPECS Framework and reflect on previous choices; why you made them, and the consequences of the choices.
- Consider aspects of the SPECS Framework and see where the issues and/or gaps are to learn from and improve future choices.

Consider what is important to you now

- Ask questions around the aspect of the SPECS Framework that is most important to you now.
- Ask questions around all the aspects of the SPECS Framework.

Imagine the future

- Imagine a future situation and consider each aspect of the SPECS Framework.
- Take one of the aspects of the SPECS Framework and prepare yourself for the future.

Self-confidence

Sometimes we are confident and sometimes we are over-confident. Often we have a tendency to lack confidence and this has a critical impact on the choices we make.

We can think
- There are others better than me
- I am sure to fail
- It is too hard, I will not bother
- I am frightened they will find me out
- I am not good enough
- I think I never know enough

We can also think
- I can easily do that
- I am really good at this
- Whatever I do is fine
- I cannot fail
- I feel good because I achieved that

Consider how self-confidence influences your choices.

The negative voice can block the best choices

Sometimes the voice in our head is loud. Often it is negative. It tells us negative comments that can stop us from making our best choices.

These comments often come from the mind-bricks created from a difficult situation or someone saying something negative about us.

We have a choice to listen or to ignore this voice.

The choice to listen to or ignore the negative voice in our head is influenced by our mind-bricks.

To make the best choices, choose what to listen to and what to ignore.

Exercise: What would you do?

Imagine you are offered two jobs. One you feel confident you can do and one you do not. Of course, there are other factors including money, location, and the people you will be working with, but what do you think your tendency will be?

Do you take the easy or the challenging job?

Notice your tendency.

Tendencies impact on choices.

We make better choices when we are self-confident

Sometimes we have to find courage to overcome our lack of confidence.

When we do this, it makes us feel better about ourselves and we are more likely to make better choices.

Self-confidence impacts on your choices.

Whatever problems come, face them boldly and with self-confidence.

Have the confidence that whatever happens is for your own good and develop a positive way of thinking.

Spiritual Teacher

Self-confidence in business

There are different aspects of self-confidence in business, including the confidence of the owner and senior executives, individuals in the company, internal teams, and the business as an entity.

Owners, leaders, and entrepreneurs

There are leaders who are self-confident, make choices collaboratively and have the knowledge, skills and experience to make the best choices.

These people have a track record of making the best choices and do not tend to have a voice in their head that tells them negative comments. They are clear about the vision, values, and strategy and take the appropriate amount of time to make choices.

Individuals

Individuals who are clear about what is expected of them and are trained, motivated, supported, and valued tend to be more engaged and self-confident than those who are not. They make the best choices.

Teams

High-performing teams collaborate, share knowledge and experience, and support each other. They have skilled managers who listen and understand, provide direction and support, and make choices that create high performance.

Organisations

If an organisation has had a difficult time and needs to perform better, it needs a strategy that will support achieving results. This requires clarity around the vision, values, key objectives, and what is working well and what is not. To deliver high performance, there needs to be capable and skilled people and added value products and services. When all this is in place and working well, the company becomes high performing and profitable, and that increases business confidence.

Confident businesses make the best choices.

Five reflective questions – Self-confidence

○ Remember a situation when you have been self-confident. How did you feel?

○ What do you think others would notice about you if you were more self-confident?

○ What would change the most in your life if you had more self-confidence?

○ What choices would you make if you were more self-confident?

○ What key actions do you need to do now to increase your self-confidence?

Self-confidence: a quick summary

○ Consider whether you are limiting your choices because of either feeling over-confident, or not feeling confident enough.

○ If you lack self-confidence, notice and explore it.

○ Watch and see how self-confidence impacts on your choices.

○ If you can do something to increase your confidence, do it now.

Self-confidence impacts on your choices.

Stop acting
so small.
You are
the universe
in ecstatic
motion.

Rumi

Processing

Processing is the structure and method by which you make and understand choices. It is the what and how of making choices.

There are numerous ways to make choices. Each of us has our own way. Here are some typical examples of how we make choices.

- The way we think
- The feelings we have
- Only listening to ourselves
- Asking lots of people
- Doing lots of research
- Gut reactions
- Considering past experiences
- Seeing many choices and getting confused
- Being easily influenced by other people
- Influenced by our hopes and fears
- Slow or fast choices

- Impulsive choices
- Hesitant choices that can mean missed opportunities
- A tendency to worry about how others think
- A tendency to not want to upset anyone

Notice the way you are processing your choice-making and consider how that impacts on your choices.

Some choices are more complex to make than others and you need to spend more time gathering information and analysing to inform your choice.

If you have a way to make choices that works for you, keep it.

If you want to explore processing in another way, change it.

Changing the process of making your choices can produce a different and potentially better choice.

Examples of types of business choices

- Minor
- Complex
- Day-to-day
- Routine
- Operational
- Major change
- Strategic
- Critical
- Not important now
- Analytical
- Short-term
- Long-term
- Tactical
- Logical
- In your control
- Out of your control

Leadership requires making a myriad of choices about the business

- You as a leader
- Leaders and managers
- Partners
- Customers
- Resources

- Risk management
- The impact on other divisions
- The impact on people
- The impact on customers
- New products and services
- Research and development
- Innovation and creativity
- Salary structures
- Personal issues
- Emotional upsets
- Health
- Organisational structure
- Behaviours and values
- Developing staff
- Succession
- Legal and regulatory requirements
- Ethics
- Marketing
- Leadership and management
- Getting new business
- Prioritising
- Time
- Meetings

Different approaches to making choices

- Fast
- Reactive
- Considered
- Researched
- Slow
- Considering the pros and cons
- Monitoring trends
- Rating the most attractive and least attractive choice
- Sleeping on it
- Emotionally
- Collaboratively
- On your own
- Learning from past experiences
- With peace and calm
- Away from home or the office
- Learning from other people's choices
- Choosing from a wide range of choices
- Limiting the number of choices
- Instinctively
- Without thinking
- When it feels right
- Testing a choice out first before making the final choice

- In a quiet place
- In a learning environment
- Talking to friends
- Talking to other people in a similar field
- In teams
- Taking exercise
- Taking time out
- Leaving it until it is necessary
- Learning from other experiences
- Waiting to the last minute
- When other choices have been made
- When circumstances have changed
- Deciding not to make the choice
- Logically
- Analytically
- Intuitively
- On a regular basis
- Creatively

Do you want to change your choice-making process?

If so, then consider:

- the way you tend to make choices; and
- a different approach.

Notice what choice-making process works well for you and consider if you want to change the process and make choices differently.

Always think
for some time
before taking
any important
action and
slowly do what is
necessary, with
a peaceful and
calm mind.

Spiritual Teacher

The process of focusing

Wherever you focus your mind that is where your mind is. Focus is a choice.

When you focus on the negative, you will see negative. When you focus on the positive, you will see positive.

When you are considering purchasing a particular model of car, you will find yourself focusing on that model whenever you are around cars.

At work, when you are focused on performance targets, most of your choices are around making sure the targets are achieved.

If you want to make a different choice you can shift your focus.

When you shift your focus, you can shift your choices.

Change does not happen in isolation

When we make a choice, it nearly always has an impact on something or someone else. It causes a change.

When making a choice, you need to consider what the potential impact of that change will be for now and potentially in the future.

Identifying potential knock-on reactions to choices can be difficult because sometimes it is not clear what the impact is, especially if there are constant changes.

It may require discussions with other people who understand how the choice can impact on their situation.

In business and government, we see how the impact of choices is not always fully considered. A choice may work successfully in one area, but may cause significant issues elsewhere.

Choices can cause change and change does not happen in isolation.

Business scenario

A business chose to introduce individual performance-related bonuses. Everyone had a personal target to achieve the bonus.

The company found that by choosing individual performance-related bonuses, people were motivated and met one of the company's objectives.

However, people's focus on the process of achieving personal targets resulted in less focus on some of the other key team and company objectives.

When evaluating the performance-related bonus, it was recognised that the individual performance-related bonus was not fully effective.

This company is now considering an alternative choice or a different process.

Five reflective questions – Processing

- In what ways do you usually make choices?
- Remember some of your best choices, how did you make them?
- Do you want to make changes to your choice-making process?
- What needs to change if you want to make choices differently?
- What is your focus now?

Processing: a quick summary

- Notice your habits and patterns when making choices
- Notice your focus because it drives your choices
- If your process works, keep it; if not, change it
- If you change the process of making choices, it can change the choices
- Consider how your choices can impact on other people and situations

Expression

We spend many years throughout our lives developing and cultivating our unique personalities and we want to express it in many and varied ways.

We express ourselves to other people and to ourselves by the way we:

- Dress
- Use body language
- Speak, sing, cook, paint
- Listen
- Behave
- Have relationships
- Drive, write, speak
- Behave at parties
- Treat our friends and family
- Help our community
- Decorate our homes
- Tell people about our dreams

- Share our stories
- Demonstrate our talents
- Parent our children
- Live our values
- Share our innermost feelings
- Talk to people
- Share our views
- Vote
- Lead our businesses
- Manage people

Everything we do is an expression of our personality.

Expression enhances clarity

Some people have difficulty in expressing themselves because of their mind-bricks.

They may not be able to express what they think because they find it difficult to think clearly or find language challenging.

They may not be able to express their feelings because they have a brick that says, 'do not express your feelings.'

This can be from conditioned thinking, past experiences, fear, the way they have been taught, a habit, lack of clarity, or a difficulty in communicating with people.

These people will benefit from working with other people and enhancing their communication skills and focusing more on their feelings.

When we express our thoughts and feelings clearly, we feel better and other people understand us better.

With clarity we make better choices.

Expression in business

Successful businesses make choices and understand how to express them internally and externally.

Internally

○ Choices are clearly communicated so that everyone understands

○ Managers express themselves through their behaviours aligned with the organisation's values and culture

○ There is a style of expression unique to the business

○ The look and feel of the environment expresses the company's brand

○ People express their ideas, issues, and passions

Externally

○ The brand expresses what the business is about to the outside world

○ External people perceive the business in the way the business wants to be perceived

Leaders who express compassion can create high-performing people and teams

- When leaders choose to judge their employees and say critical and often hurtful comments, they do not develop high-performing people. Instead they have frightened people who do not tell the leaders what is really happening, and usually they want to leave.

- When leaders do not listen and involve people, they have an incomplete view of what is happening in their business. This lack of knowledge impacts on their choices.

- Compassionate leaders are nurturing, caring, and forgiving. Their people feel part of the business and together they make considered choices.

Compassionate leaders make choices that are more likely to achieve high-performance.

Courtesy, generosity, honesty, persistence, and kindness. If you are courteous, you will not be disrespected. If you are generous,

you will gain
everything. If
you are honest,
people will rely
on you. If you
are persistent,
you will get
results. If you are
kind, you can
employ people.

Confucius

Understand other people's mind-bricks

Through our expression, we want to be heard. But not just heard; heard in a way we *want* to be heard.

However, that is not necessarily the way other people hear us because they are filtering through their own mind-bricks.

Making choices in collaboration can be powerful, yet sometimes we are misheard by other people who can only hear themselves. This can result in miscommunication and confusion.

Millions of people are constantly miscommunicating and this impacts on their choices. It causes breakdowns in relationships, arguments in business and a huge amount of upset.

To make the best choices, we need to express ourselves in the way people understand. This requires understanding other people's mind-bricks.

Express yourself in a way that people understand.

Five reflective questions – Expression

○ What is most important about expression to you?

○ How could your life be different if you expressed yourself in other ways?

○ What could you choose to do to express yourself differently?

○ How would others see you if you expressed yourself differently?

○ Is there anything you need to do now to change the way you express yourself?

Expression: a quick summary

○ Notice how you express yourself and whether you want to make changes

○ When you feel it is right, check out some of the miscommunications that may have caused you problems in the past

○ Choose to express yourself in ways that other people will understand

○ Leaders who express compassion are more likely to achieve high-performance

Connectivity

Our mind-bricks can make us feel disconnected.

We do not always trust people. When we meet a new person we can compare ourselves to them. Sometimes we can compete with people who are close to us.

Yet everyone longs to feel connected at some level. We do not want to feel we are separate and need to protect ourselves.

When we are connected we belong, we feel held.

There is a feeling of being loved.

We can connect in many ways

- Our inner self
- Family, friends, partners
- People we respect
- Employees
- Nature
- People who make us laugh
- People who have high-standing in our communities
- People who tell us we are great
- People who can help us
- Colleagues and bosses who have higher status
- People who make us feel better about ourselves
- People who are fun to be with
- People who we can trust with our innermost feelings
- People who we can gossip with
- People who say things we want to say, but are too scared to say them
- Art
- Objects we enjoy
- People we can treat like heroes
- Our pets and people who love their pets

- People who give us a sense of meaning and purpose
- People who reward us in some way
- Our thoughts, beliefs and feelings, religions
- Sport
- Entertainment
- Our bodies
- Our past
- Our ancestors
- Where we live
- Our countries
- Our feelings
- Other human beings in the universe
- Our moods
- Music
- Money
- Jobs we do
- Our homes
- Books
- Our position in society
- Our faith
- Our communities
- Our ideas

Connectivity in business

- Our teams
- Existing clients
- Partners
- Board members
- Partnerships
- Potential new clients
- Products and services
- Networking events
- Social media
- Technology
- Surveys and research
- Seminars and exhibitions
- Lunches
- Business groups
- Entertaining
- Sales and marketing
- Public relations
- Stakeholder engagement
- Shareholder relations
- Websites, webinars, newsletters
- Meetings

Connectivity and mind-bricks

To connect with other people socially or in business, we need to understand their mind-bricks. We also need to connect to our mind-bricks.

When we are connected to our mind-bricks, we have a better understanding of which choices to make.

Often we make choices to help us be more connected.

On a deeper level we can see that everyone and everything is connected in some way.
There is a shared energy beyond our mind-bricks that connects everything.

Five reflective questions – Connectivity

- What is most important about connectivity to you now?
- How could your life be different if you connected differently?
- What do you need to do to be better connected?
- Is there anything stopping you being better connected?
- What one thing could you do now to make a difference to your connectivity?

Connectivity: a quick summary

- We all naturally tend to feel disconnected at some level
- We all want to feel more connected
- Notice what you are connected to now
- Notice how you are disconnected
- Consider how connectivity impacts on your choices

Learn how to see. Realise that everything connects to everything else.

Leonardo da Vinci

Security

Our basic instinct is to protect our mind-bricks, and
security is fundamental.

Most people do not purposefully put themselves
into a situation where they are insecure because it
is frightening.

However, there are times when risks need to be
taken. These choices are not easy to make.

*Notice how security impacts on making your
choice.*

Mind-bricks can create fear

Most people live in their mind-bricks of thoughts and often there is fear. This can come from past experience, the present situation, or fear of the future.

Fear comes in many ways including fear of loss, failure, blame, shame, mistakes, losing business, conflict, looking stupid, rejection, insecurity, change, and death.

We make choices filtered through our mind-bricks of fear. Often we do not notice when it is fear making the choice. Ultimately, we are protecting our personalities.

Sometimes fear is helpful because it is a positive warning. Often fear is negative and holds us back from making the best choices.

Of course, fear is not easy to overcome, but it is helpful to recognise the irrational fears by watching the mind. Once the fear is recognised, the choices will be different.

Notice your fears so you can make your best choices.

All power is within you: you can do anything and everything. Believe in that, do not believe that you are weak. Stand up and express the divinity within you.

Swami Vivekananda

Examples of individual security

- Close relationships
- Financial robustness
- A secure job
- A place we can call home
- Good health
- Having most of the things we want
- Freedom to live as we want in a stable country
- Being in a safe neighbourhood
- A sense of having control
- A good education for our children
- A safe lock on the door
- Politicians who are fair and just
- A passport to travel if we want to
- People who can take care of us if we need it
- An affordable medical system
- Affordable food
- Being around people who are like-minded

Examples of security in business

- Effective leadership and management
- Skilled and motivated people
- Strong turnover and profit
- The desired amount of customers and clients
- Financial resources and robust financial management
- Knowledge and expertise
- The right number and spread of clients
- Clear vision and direction
- Regular risk monitoring
- Insurances
- Intellectual property if appropriate
- Affordable offices in the right location
- A secure marketplace
- Competitive advantage
- Continual adding value
- Sustainability
- Succession plan
- Regular risk management
- High-performing teams
- Effective partnerships
- Clear strategic/business plans

Choices for managing risk

- ○ Mitigate/reduce the risk - reducing the probability of the risk occurring with regular risk planning and monitoring
- ○ Accept the risk – nothing can be done
- ○ Transfer the risk – for instance outsource to a third party
- ○ Avoid the risk – change the strategy

The Choiceables®
Risk Management Table

Identify the risk	
Consider the potential impact	
Rate level of risk: high, medium, low	
Risk choice strategy • Mitigate/reduce • Accept • Transfer • Avoid	
Expected risk date	
Risk monitoring dates	
Who is responsible for managing risk?	

Five reflective questions – Security

- What is most important about security to you now?
- When have you felt most secure?
- How could your life be different if you did not have fear?
- On a scale of 1-10, how secure do you feel?
- What choices do you need to make to increase your level of security?

Security: a quick summary

- Security is a basic instinct influenced by our mind-bricks
- Fear can be a positive warning or it can be a block
- Notice when fear is talking
- Most people consider security when making a choice
- Security is a key driver of choices

Examples of questions for businesses using the SPECS Framework

Self-confidence

- Do people have self-confidence?
- Do we include people enough when we make choices?
- Do our leaders and managers have confidence in their own capabilities?
- Do our leaders and managers help make people feel confident?
- What can we do to increase people's self-confidence?

Processing

- Are our processes and systems working well?
- Have we got the best process for making choices?
- Is our communication process working?
- Can we improve the way we develop strategies and plans?
- What else can we do better to make our processes work for us?

Expression

- Do we express our brand in the way we want to be perceived?
- Do potential clients understand our products and services?
- Do we have the values that accurately express and reflect who we are and want to be? Do we live by them?
- How can we be more creative and innovative?
- Does our location and office express who we are?

Connectivity

- Are we connected to the right external stakeholders i.e. clients, important people, and organisations?
- How connected are we as a management team?
- Have we connected our vision with our values and objectives?
- Do we collaborate in our teams and as a company?
- Do people connect and treat each other with compassion?

Security

- Do we have the financial and non-financial resources we need to achieve our objectives?
- Can we manage risk better?
- Are we getting the results we need?
- Do we have the professional support we need?
- Are we creating value to increase our security i.e. intellectual property?

The SPECS Framework
Action Table

SPECS	Issues	Choices	Activities	Timing	How will we know we are successful?	Who is responsible?
Self-confidence						
Processing						
Expression						
Connectivity						
Security						

How to do step two

Looking outside and questioning

You can ask questions around a selection of the five words in SPECS or complete all of the framework. Select the word you want to start with and ask yourself what it means to you now.

Notice that responses to each of the five considerations are likely to change according to different situations. This impacts on your choices.

By asking questions around the SPECS Framework, your choice will become clearer.

BEING WITHIN

Focusing on
being within,
beyond thought,
where there is
an inner stillness
and knowing.

Being within,
choices are clear.

Looking Outside and Being Within

We tend to look outside of ourselves most of the time. When we look outside, there can be desire and fear; there is an expectation of an outcome. These expectations are thoughts about the future. Sometimes we get the outcome we want and sometimes we do not. When we do not get what we want, we are disappointed. We can also get angry. This disturbs our mind and impacts our choices.

Yet we can take a moment to watch our thoughts as though they are separate from us. When you watch, there will be a distance from your thoughts.

This will help you calm your mind and go beyond thinking about the past and future. You will be present. With a calm mind you will make clearer choices.

Beyond thinking there is a place of stillness and peace that we all have within us.

A calm mind makes better choices.

Look at
your mind
dispassionately -
this is enough to
calm it. When it
is quiet you can
go beyond it.
Do not keep busy
all the time. Stop
it and just be.

Sri Nisargadatta Maharaj

We all have inner knowing

When we are being within it is a different way to live.

We are less externally focused and more internally focused.

We can be behind our thoughts and connect with the great stillness within.

In this space there is inner knowing.

We can use thinking as an amazing tool. However, we are more than our thoughts.

When there is stillness, beyond thoughts, we do not need to protect ourselves from other people who we think are separate from us. There is no worry about the past or anxiety about the future. We are present.

There is compassion, love, peace and no fear.

We are being within.

We all have this inner knowing. It is a choice to be within.

We are more than our thoughts

If we allow ourselves to stop and be still, we can know ourselves beyond our thinking and personality.

Spiritual teachers say our mind is like an empty screen. On this screen we project thoughts of names, images, fears, memories, labels, forms and concepts. Each person has their own film showing their unique personality.

The screen in the background remains and everything else on it changes. Within this unchanging screen and without the film we are being within.

We tend to associate ourselves with the thinking projections and not with the being within. When we are being within, we are aware that we are always connected with the constant stillness.

There is a pure inner knowing.

Being within, choices are clear.

A quiet mind does not mean that there will be no thoughts or mental movements, but that these will be on the surface, and you will feel your true being within, separate from them, observing but not carried away.

Sri Aurobindo

Recommended books written by spiritual teachers

The Power of Now: A Guide to Spiritual Enlightenment by Eckhart Tolle

I Am That by Maharaj Sri Nisargadatta

The Essential Rumi translated by Coleman Barks

The Miracle of Mindfulness by Thich Nhat Hanh

The Quiet Mind: Sayings of the White Eagle

An Open Heart by The Dalai Lama

Practical exercises
to help you
make choices

Meditation calms the mind and helps to make better choices

One purpose of meditation is to slow down the thoughts and take you into the being within state. This is the state beyond thought where there is stillness and peace. One way to do this is to focus on watching your breath. This will shift your focus from thinking and take you into the stillness.

When your mind has a thought, allow it to pass and gently bring the focus back to your breath. This will slow your thoughts and help you to be still.

You might like to sit in a quiet place with your eyes closed. This place can be kept as your regular meditation space.

When you practise, you will discover the way that suits you. Regular practice will make a difference to your mind. Slowly, your focus will shift more towards the inner quiet.

Meditation is an ongoing practice.

Listen without judgment

Consider the reason why you want to make a choice and some of the most important questions you want to ask yourself about that choice. You can write this down and put the paper aside.

Then sit quietly. You can do this with your eyes closed if preferred.

Receive the responses to the questions as they come to you without judging them. Keep asking the questions and writing the responses down afterwards if you prefer.

You can also draw pictures instead of words, or create pictures and words. You can find insightful feedback with yourself this way.

What choice would your inner guide make?

Ask yourself what choice would your inner guide, goodness, love or wise person make?

Daily writing

Choose a writing book and leave it by your bed. Each day when you wake up, write anything that comes into your mind. No judging or correcting, just write. This can clear your mind as though you are clearing a desk. Try it for a week and see whether this works for you and continue if it does. A clearer mind makes better choices.

Move the body

Exercising your body by going out for a walk, running, yoga, sport or dancing can take your mind away from thinking. This allows your mind some space. It is likely after exercising you will find you have a clearer mind from which to make your choice.

Take time out

It is helpful to have a rest from making the choice so when you return there is new energy and clarity. This also works well when making choices in a workshop or in a meeting.

Listen to music

To bring a fresh approach to making your choice, you can listen to music you love, to calm your thoughts.

Sleep on it

When you have a challenging choice, delay making the choice until you are ready. Many people find after they have had a good sleep, their choices are clearer when they wake up.

Gratitude

With love and gratitude to all my spiritual teachers.

I also thank my mother, Simon, Anya, Joel, Simona, Eunice, Heidi, Reina, Michael and Natalie.

And thank you to all my wonderful friends, family, colleagues, and clients who have taught me much in varied and beautiful ways.

With appreciation to my book coach, Wendy Yorke and also to designer, Gareth Hobbs. Their support was invaluable.

looking inside

looking outside

being within

reflect

thinking

question

be

beyond thinking

MIND-BRICKS

The bricks that make up your life now. Your thoughts, feelings, memories, conditioning. Your personality.

Choices are made according to your mind-bricks.

SPECS FRAMEWORK

Self-confidence
Processing
Expression
Connectivity
Security

The only five considerations for making any choice.

BEING WITHIN

Focusing on being within, beyond thought, where there is an inner stillness and knowing.

Being within, choices are clear.

A final word about the Choiceables Model

The Choiceables Model has three steps: looking inside, looking outside, and being within.

Looking inside, we reflect on our thoughts and consider why, what, and how our choices are influenced.

Looking outside, we question using the SPECS Framework, which is a mnemonic for the only five considerations we need to make any choice.

Being within, we align with the wisdom of our inner stillness, beyond thought. In this space, there is a calm mind from which to make choices.

You can use the steps separately, mix elements of the steps, or use all three steps together. It is not fixed.

I hope the Choiceables Model helps you to gain fresh insights that will enable you to make the best choices.

Andrea

All the powers in the universe are already ours. It is we who have put our hands before our eyes and cry that it is dark.

Swami Vivekananda

Andrea Defries

Andrea is an insightful, practical and creative business consultant and coach. She started her career in sales and marketing in a large multi-national company, and then moved into consulting mostly working with owners and senior managers in small and medium sized businesses.

She helps clients to see the big picture, view issues from different perspectives and focus on what is important. Her aim is to help clients to think differently and find simple solutions to achieve their vision and goals.

Andrea's work is informed from integrating over 20 years of working with leaders helping them to make choices and a lifetime's personal enquiry including learning from spiritual teachers.

It is with this fusion of business and spiritual learning that she has developed a unique model for making the best choices in life and business. It's called Choiceables®.

Contacting Andrea Defries

Andrea is the Founder of The Happy Business Consultancy based in London. She provides a range of services to help leaders make choices and enhance their businesses. This includes coaching, training and workshops. For more information about working with Andrea, please visit www.thehappybusiness.co.uk

Lightning Source UK Ltd.
Milton Keynes UK
UKOW06f0459130917
309102UK00009B/85/P